D1016969

Style

and illustrations by Alison Oliver

y Lambeth Hochwald

hed in the United States by Potter
an imprint of the Crown Publishing
a division of Random House, Inc.,
rk.

arksonpotter.com
d in China

978-0-307-71979-9

This journal belongs t

...and

Pot

Des:
Tex
Copy
Publ
Styl
Grou
New

www.
Prin

ISBN

Potter
Style

mom manifesto

I'm a mom so I know how hard it is to find five seconds to make sure your lipstick is on straight, let alone eke out a few moments to record your thoughts. But instead of requiring you to write long, detailed posts, this journal aims to help you capture all those fleeting thoughts *quickly* and *easily* whether you're in the midst of pushing your stroller down the street or waiting for your child to finish a piano lesson. The goal: you'll end up with a book of memories—big and small—that make up your life as a mom.

Keep in mind that you don't have to follow the prompts chronologically—just pick up the journal and find a topic that speaks to you most at that moment. And don't feel guilty if you neglect it for a few weeks or even months. You can always pick up where you left off, no problem. Also, feel free to elaborate on any of the prompts. Whatever you do, keep this journal close at hand.

Please note: this is an equal-opportunity book for all of us moms. Whether you're married, remarried or dating, have one child or ten, live in a small town or a big city this journal is for you.

Happy journaling. Make it yours!
—Lambeth, mother of Zachary, age 6

Since I've become a parent, I have been able to sleep late _____ days a week.

My ideal Sunday morning includes:

☐ Brunch at a greasy spoon

☐ Sunday talk shows

☐ Sunday newspaper

☐ A morning walk

☐ Waffles for the kids

☐ Cuddling and watching cartoons

☐ The gym

☐ Other: _____

Notes: _____

_____

_____

_____

_____

DATE: ___/___/___

How I rank the following:

	NOT MY CUP OF TEA	SO-SO	MUST HAVE!
A signature fragrance			
Coffee			
Crossword puzzles			
Diamond earrings			
Drive-throughs			
Flannel PJs			
The library			
Personal trainer			
Recycling			
Spanx			
Springtime			
Road trips			

Reading bedtime stories is one of my favorite parts about being a mom. I love telling friends about these five kids' books:

1. _____

2. _____

3. _____

4. _____

5. _____

BONUS: Here's the best story my parents ever read

to me: _____

_____

_____

_____

_____

The best thing about having a child is that I've gotten to:

☐ Spend long days at the zoo

☐ Rediscover my love for animal crackers

☐ Wander endlessly in toy stores

☐ Tap into my multitasking abilities.
  I'm good at this mommying thing!

☐ Other:

_____

_____

_____

_____

_____

_____

_____

_____

_____ is a friend
with whom I've lost touch that I've missed
the most.

Why: _____

_____

_____

_____

_____

_____ is a friend
with whom I've lost touch that I've missed
the least.

Why: _____

_____

_____

_____

_____

DATE: ___ / ___ / ___

Today, my mood is:

☐ Blissed out

☐ Ticked off

☐ Wiped out

☐ SOS, send chocolate

☐ Other: _____

_____

_____

_____

Here's why: _____

_____

_____

_____

_____

_____

Five ways my significant other and I
chill out:

We watch our favorite show:_____

_____

We listen to our favorite band:_____

_____

We engage in energetic games of:_____

_____

_____

We look at old videos of:_____

_____

_____

We make our favorite meal of:_____

_____

_____

_____

DATE: _____ / _____ / _____

My idea of a great way to unwind:

☐ Brew another pot of coffee

☐ Draw a bubble bath

☐ Call a friend

☐ Read a magazine

☐ Snuggle with anyone, even if the only one awake is the cat

☐ Other: _____

_____

_____

_____

_____

_____

_____

_____

_____

Today_____ mostly made
(child's name)
this face:

Because _____
_____
_____
_____
_____

DATE: _____ / _____ / _____

Today I mostly made this face:

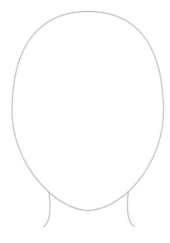

Because _____

_____

_____

_____

_____

_____ has an amazing
(child's name)
imagination. Here's one crazy story that I
don't want to forget:

_____

_____

_____

_____

_____

_____

_____

_____

_____

_____

_____

_____

DATE: / /

Last night I had a dream that:

_____

_____

_____

_____

_____

_____

_____

_____

_____

_____

_____

_____

_____

_____

_____

I've gotta get my mojo back. Choose one (or all five) of the following mantras to repeat:

- [ ] I will snuggle on the couch with my significant other without thinking about the Pirate's Booty stuck in between the cushions.

- [ ] I will find—and wear—sexy bras!

- [ ] I will invite my significant other to take a bath with me even if all we have is Dora-themed bubble bath.

- [ ] When my significant other rubs my back, I will allow my mind to drift to that pre-baby trip to Jamaica, not to all the bills that need to be paid.

- [ ] I will light candles in our bedroom in the hopes that the mood moves us.

BONUS: Invent your own mantra here:

_____

_____

_____

DATE: ___ / ___ / ___

I think _____ would make
       (child's name)
a great:

☐ Scientist   ☐ Opera singer

☐ Mediator   ☐ Nurse

☐ Musician   ☐ Teacher

☐ Entrepreneur   ☐ Mystery writer

☐ Farmer   ☐ Makeup artist

☐ Banker   ☐ Other: _____

☐ Mechanic   _____

☐ Palm reader   _____

Because _____

_____

_____

_____

_____

In a fire, I'd grab: _____

_____

_____

_____

In a fire, I think my kid(s) would grab:

_____

_____

_____

Notes: _____

_____

_____

_____

_____

DATE: _____ / _____ / _____

When I make _____'s
                    (child's name)
school lunch, I go all out. Checklist of things
I always include:

☐ Something homemade   ☐ A sweet treat

☐ A heart-shaped note from me ☐ A piece of fruit

☐ Other: _____

Not me. When I think of school lunch:

☐ I'd rather just give them the lunch money.

☐ I got lucky! It may always be PB&J but

_____ always makes lunch.
          (child's name)

And let's face it, my kid generally:

☐ eats the whole lunch   ☐ trades half

☐ tosses everything but dessert

BONUS: When I was in school, I remember having

_____ for lunch.

The things I love about our neighborhood:

☐ The people

☐ The style of homes

☐ The trees

☐ The way everyone pitches in to keep it
looking nice

☐ The fact that all the parents watch the
kids—even if their own child is inside.

☐ Being so close to_____

☐ Being so far from_____

☐ Other:_____

_____

_____

_____

_____

_____

DATE: _____ / _____ / _____

The things I hate about our neighborhood:

☐ The people

☐ The noise

☐ The way every other house has a plastic
swing set in the yard

☐ The fact that the parents keep to themselves—
even after I brought everyone homemade pie
upon moving in

☐ The lack of nice playgrounds

☐ Being so close to _____

☐ Being so far from _____

☐ Other: _____

_____

_____

_____

_____

_____

I'll never forget the worst fight my significant other and I ever had. We actually went to bed without speaking. It took us _____ hours to apologize.

My takeaway: _____

_____

_____

_____

_____

My partner's takeaway (I hope): _____

_____

_____

_____

_____

_____

DATE: _____ / _____ / _____

The most embarrassing thing I've done to date
when I've been short on cash:

☐ Emptied my kid's piggybank

☐ Rolled quarters

☐ Borrowed from my line of credit

☐ Asked my in-laws for money

☐ Other:_____

Notes:_____

_____

_____

_____

_____

_____

_____

_____ loves an imaginary
(child's name)
friend named _____. Here's
everything you need to know about him/her:

_____

_____

_____

_____

_____

_____

I...

☐ had an imaginary friend once. I was _____ years
old and this is what I remember about him/her:

_____

_____

_____

☐ Nope. I never had an imaginary friend.

DATE: _____ / _____ / _____

When I think back to the moment I walked down the aisle at my wedding, these are some of the first thoughts to come to mind:

My dress was: _____

_____

My hair was: _____

_____

My shoes were: _____

_____

I felt:

☐ Intensely happy   ☐ Hot

☐ Exhausted   ☐ Bossy

☐ Weepy   ☐ Like a celebrity

☐ In a daze   ☐ Other: _____

_____

_____

Even though we're parents, we've had some
pretty memorable nights out like:

☐ A couples' massage at a spa

☐ Dinner and a late movie

☐ A night at a hotel

☐ A concert and a decadent chocolate dessert at
the hippest place in town

☐ Other:_____

_____

Notes:_____

_____

_____

_____

_____

_____

DATE: _____ / _____ / _____

Our favorite seasonal family activities are:

Spring: _____

_____

_____

Summer: _____

_____

_____

Fall: _____

_____

_____

Winter:_____

_____

_____

Right now, _____ looks
(child's name)
more like me in this way:

_____

_____

_____

_____

_____

_____

Right now, _____ looks
(child's name)
more like my significant other in this way:

_____

_____

_____

_____

_____

DATE: _____ / _____ / _____

Right now, _____ acts
                    (child's name)
more like me in this way:

_____

_____

_____

_____

_____

_____

Right now, _____ acts
                    (child's name)
more like my significant other in this way:

_____

_____

_____

_____

_____

_____

When I read parenting books, I want to:

☐ Cry

☐ Laugh

☐ Sneer

☐ Barf

☐ Yell

☐ Call my college roommate

☐ Reach for the remote

☐ Other: _____

The best I've read: _____

_____

_____

...and the worst: _____

_____

_____

Honesty alert! If I want to truly examine my
behavior, I'd say that I:

	NEVER	ALWAYS
Am on time		
Remember birthdays		
Am open to meeting new people		
Pay my bills on time		
Say sorry first		
Send a thank-you note		
Manage my time well		
Tell the truth about my age		
Ask good questions		
Interrupt		

The thing I love most about my marriage:

_____

_____

_____

_____

_____

The thing I love least about my marriage:

_____

_____

_____

_____

_____

DATE: _____ / _____ / _____

I want to throw a cool parents dinner party.
Here's what I'm going to serve:

Beverages:_____

_____

Appetizer:_____

_____

Entrée:_____

_____

Dessert:_____

_____

Here's the guest list:_____

_____

_____

_____

_____

_____

Right now, I'm worried most about (rank these on a scale of 1 to 5, with 1 being the most important):

☐ Global warming

☐ How my kids are being educated

☐ Paying for college

☐ Keeping my house from looking like a hurricane hit

☐ The fact that I can't keep my eyes open past 9 PM

Other things that make me a certifiable

worrywart_____

_____

_____

_____

_____

So maybe I sported Sally Jessy Raphael glasses when I was eight. I don't ever want my child to feel *that* uncool. Here are five ways I'll boost his or her confidence:

1. _____

2. _____

3. _____

4. _____

5. _____

Here are five more uncool things about me when I was a kid:

1. _____

2. _____

3. _____

4. _____

5. _____

My significant other and I laugh the most
when we think of:

_____

_____

_____

_____

_____

_____

_____

_____

_____

_____

_____

_____

_____

_____

The one thing I remember my parents saying about my significant other when they met for the first time:

_____

_____

_____

_____

_____

The one thing I remember my friends saying about my significant other when they met for the first time:

_____

_____

_____

_____

_____

Something wonderful that I learned from my kid(s) today:

_____

_____

_____

_____

_____

_____

_____

_____

_____

_____

_____

_____

DATE: _____ / _____ / _____

How much time I devote to the following:

	HARDLY ANY	HERE AND THERE	LOTS!
Naps			
TV			
Dessert			
Laughter			
Banter			
Art			
Retail therapy			
Vacation planning			
Work			
Carpooling			
Googling			
eBay			

I may never live in it, but my dream
home looks like this:

Location:_____

How many bedrooms:_____

Color scheme:_____

I'd most love to live:

☐ By the ocean   ☐ In the rainforest

☐ In the mountains   ☐ In a big city

My house would be a:

☐ Victorian   ☐ Cabin

☐ Farmhouse   ☐ Minimal apartment
                               on the 40th floor
☐ Tree House
                             ☐ Other:
☐ Houseboat

_____

_____

_____

DATE: _____ / _____ / _____

My scale is:

☐ Covered in dust

☐ Covered with a year's worth of magazines

☐ Something I live to please

☐ The bane of my existence

☐ Other: _____

And this is how I feel about it: _____

_____

_____

_____

_____

_____

_____

_____

_____

The most memorable family vacation I took as
a kid was to _____.
I was _____ years old.

Why it was memorable:

_____

_____

_____

_____

_____

_____

_____

_____

_____

_____

_____

_____

_____

DATE: _____ / _____ / _____

The most memorable family vacation we've
taken yet was to _____
Age(s) of kid(s): _____

Why it was so memorable:

_____

_____

_____

_____

_____

_____

_____

_____

BONUS: The family vacation we've yet to take but
that is the stuff of dreams:

_____

_____

_____

My Top Five Mommy (tearjerker) Moments
thus far:

_____

_____

_____

_____

_____

Top Five Double-Kleenex Moments in my future
(tag this page and come back to it):

_____

_____

_____

_____

_____

DATE: _____ / _____ / _____

My kid said what?

I can't even believe_____
(child's name)

said_____

_____

_____.

We were_____.
(activity/location)

My child is only_____ years old.

More notes on the matter:_____

_____

_____

_____

_____

_____

_____

_____

This is what makes my heart sing:

- [ ] The sound of a baby laughing
- [ ] My significant other's hand in mine
- [ ] The smell of roses
- [ ] The sound of my snoring dog
- [ ] The sight of the ocean (or mountains or desert)
- [ ] Other:

Notes: _____

_____

_____

_____

Other notes: _____

_____

_____

DATE: _____ / _____ / _____

When I met my significant other's family,
I was:

☐ Shocked

☐ Thrilled

☐ Concerned

☐ Happy

☐ Relieved

☐ Unsurprised

☐ Other: _____

Notes: _____

_____

_____

_____

_____

_____

If I had unlimited funds for a makeover,
I'd fix my:

☐ Hair

☐ Pores

☐ Nails

☐ Teeth

☐ Abs

☐ Breasts

☐ Other:_____

Notes:_____

_____

_____

_____

_____

_____

DATE: _____ / _____ / _____

I love watching my significant other sleeping
in the morning. Morning breath aside, the
cuteness factor is (a number between 1 and 5,
with 5 being the cutest)_____.

If the option to sleep in is there, my
significant other will usually sleep until
_____.

Notes: _____

_____

_____

_____

_____

_____

_____

_____

_____

Just say no to kiddie food!

Foods my kids eat all the time:_____

_____

Foods my kids refuse to eat:_____

_____

Foods I acquired a taste for:_____

_____

Foods I *still* haven't learned to love:_____

_____

The family dinner of my
dreams would consist of:

A.

B.   C.

DATE: _____ / _____ / _____

My house has lost its grown-up verve. Help!

I hate_____
about my living room.

The next five things I'd change about my
home are:

1. _____

2. _____

3. _____

4. _____

5. _____

Notes: _____

_____

_____

_____

_____

When I found out I was pregnant, my significant other:

- [ ] Jumped up and down for three minutes
- [ ] Kissed my stomach
- [ ] Smoked a cigar
- [ ] Called our parents
- [ ] Other: _____

Notes: _____
_____
_____
_____
_____
_____
_____
_____

DATE: ___ / ___ / ___

When I was in the delivery room, my significant other:

☐ Held my hand tight

☐ Read me love poems

☐ Passed out

☐ Twittered

☐ Other:_____

Notes:_____

_____

_____

_____

_____

_____

_____

The biggest challenges of being a mom thus far have been:

☐ Potty-training

☐ Child-proofing *everything*

☐ Sleeping through the night

☐ Getting _____ to give
    (child's name)
   up the pacifier

I've loved watching_____
                              (child's name)
learn to_____

_____

_____

_____

_____

_____

_____

DATE: /   /

The five most magical moments I have spent
with my kid(s) this year include:

1. _____

2. _____

3. _____

4. _____

5. _____

BONUS: One very unmagical moment?

_____

_____

_____

_____

_____

_____

_____

When I think of my MIL (mother-in-law)...

I'm glad that she_____.

I'm sad that she_____.

I'm mad that she_____.

My FIL (father-in-law) is _____

_____.

Notes: _____

_____

_____

_____

_____

_____

_____

_____

DATE: _____ / _____ / _____

When I think of my mother...

I'm glad that she _____ .

I'm sad that she _____ .

I'm mad that she _____ .

My father is _____

_____ .

Notes: _____

_____

_____

_____

_____

_____

_____

_____

_____

I know I can find the time to do more—even
though I feel like my schedule is jammed.
This week I plan to:

1. _____

_____

2. _____

_____

3. _____

_____

4. _____

_____

5. _____

_____

I DID IT!

_____
(signature)

_____
(date)

DATE: ___/___/___

Field trips I want to take with my kid(s):

_____

_____

_____

_____

_____

_____

And field trips I want to take with my
significant other:

_____

_____

_____

_____

_____

Five things I wish my significant other
would do more:

☐ Kiss me before the kids pile into our bed

☐ Send me sweet text

☐ Make dinner

☐ Call my mom

☐ Take charge of date night

☐ Other:_____

Notes:_____

_____

_____

_____

_____

_____

DATE: _____ / _____ / _____

Right now, my kids are making me feel:

☐ Hot and hassled

☐ Cool as a cucumber

☐ Cranky and crabby

☐ Happy as a clam

☐ Other: _____

Here's why: _____

_____

_____

_____

_____

_____

_____

_____

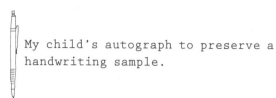

My child's autograph to preserve a
handwriting sample.

My autograph to preserve a handwriting sample.

DATE: _____ / _____ / _____

The other day, my significant other called me
"Mommy." I think that's:

☐ Super sweet

☐ Completely adorable

☐ Psychotic

☐ Freudian

☐ Other: _____

Notes: _____

_____

_____

_____

_____

_____

_____

_____

My significant other is way more generous
than I am when it comes to:

☐ Tipping

☐ Volunteering

☐ Driving

☐ Housework

☐ Presents

☐ Other:_____

This makes me feel:_____

_____

_____

_____

_____

_____

I am more generous than my significant other
when it comes to:

☐ Sharing food

☐ Chores

☐ My time

☐ Forgiveness

☐ The remote control

☐ Other:_____

This makes me feel:_____

_____

_____

_____

_____

_____

My top five iPod songs:

1. Song:_____

   Artist:_____

   This song reminds me of _____.

2. Song:_____

   Artist:_____

   This song reminds me of _____.

3. Song:_____

   Artist:_____

   This song reminds me of _____.

4. Song:_____

   Artist:_____

   This song reminds me of _____.

5. Song:_____

   Artist:_____

   This song reminds me of _____.

DATE: _____ / _____ / _____

The musicians that my kids love grooving to most during our living room dance parties:

☐ Dan Zanes

☐ Laurie Berkner

☐ Lady Gaga

☐ My old *Free to Be You and Me* sountrack

☐ Other _____

_____

_____

_____

_____

_____

_____

_____

_____

_____

I live for this dessert:_____

My favorite place to buy it/get it:_____
_____

This dessert, however, appeals to everyone on the
planet except for me:_____
_____

Notes:_____
_____
_____
_____
_____
_____
_____
_____

DATE: _____ / _____ / _____

Today's revelation:

☐ I'm not going to helicopter parent anymore.

☐ I don't care that the playroom is overrun
with Playmobil pieces and Legos.

☐ It's OK if my child wants to run around the
house in a Superman cape.

☐ I'm not going to panic now that my child
has hidden my wedding band—again.

☐ Other:_____

Here's why:_____

_____

_____

_____

_____

_____

_____ is good at making:
(child's name)

☐ Jokes

☐ Messes

☐ Art

☐ Fun (of me)

☐ Cake

☐ Up

☐ Other:_____

_____

_____

_____

_____

_____

_____

_____

DATE: _____ / _____ / _____

I'm good at making:

☐ Breakfast

☐ Music

☐ Scenes

☐ Merry

☐ Messes

☐ Peace

☐ Other:_____

_____

_____

_____

_____

_____

_____

_____

_____

The nicest thing my significant other ever
did for me pre-kids:_____

_____

_____

The nicest thing my significant other ever
did for me post-kids:_____

_____

_____

The nicest thing I ever did for my significant
other pre-kids:_____

_____

_____

The nicest thing I ever did for my significant
other post-kids:_____

_____

_____

DATE: _____ / _____ / _____

Five looks I'd like to try:

☐ A signature necklace

☐ Something low-cut but not trashy

☐ Sexy heels even if they make my feet hurt

☐ Chandelier earrings

☐ Sparkly nail polish

☐ Other:_____

_____

_____

_____

_____

_____

_____

_____

_____

_____

_____ reminds me of this

(child's name)

animal:

☐ Capuchin monkey

☐ Calico cat

☐ Yellow lab

☐ Eagle

☐ Teddy bear

☐ Horse

☐ Turtle

☐ Other:_____

Because: _____

_____

_____

_____

_____

DATE: _____ / _____ / _____

Grab the getaway car, Batman. I want to take a solo field trip alone to a:

☐ Spa

☐ Bookstore

☐ Bakery

☐ Mall

☐ Fat farm

☐ Other: _____

_____

_____

_____

_____

_____

_____

_____

_____

I'd like to meet more couples who:

☐ Have a beach house

☐ Don't compete

☐ Can avoid potentially fiery topics,
   like religion and politics

☐ Throw killer dinner parties

☐ Speak nicely to each other

☐ Can speak about other things besides the kids

☐ Haven't forgotten how to laugh—loudly—without
   being obnoxious

☐ Other: _____

_____

_____

_____

_____

_____

DATE: _____ / _____ / _____

How happy the following things make me:

	BLAH	HAPPY	ECSATIC
Chocolate ice cream			
Sleeping in			
Watching a rom-com			
Dining out			
Dancing			
Shopping			
Housework			
A great book			

If my kid(s) could have any pet in the world,
it would be a:

☐ Dog

☐ Cat

☐ Rabbit

☐ Hamster

☐ Horse

☐ Turtle

☐ Dinosaur

☐ Tarantula

☐ Unicorn

☐ Other: _____

Because: _____

_____

_____

_____

DATE: _____ / _____ / _____

The pet _____ we do have
(animal)
is named _____ .

When I think about this pet, I feel full of:

☐ Love

☐ Hate

☐ Fondness

☐ Bitterness

☐ Exhaustion

☐ Irritation

☐ Kindness

☐ Other: _____

_____

_____

_____

_____

_____

I choose what _____ wears:
(child's name)

☐ Yes

☐ No

His/her size today: _____

His/her favorite color: _____

Notes: _____

_____

_____

_____

_____

_____

_____

_____

_____

_____

Breakfast for dinner? We do it all the time.
Here are some other weekly family traditions
that I love:

_____

_____

_____

_____

_____

_____

_____

_____

_____

_____

_____

_____

_____

_____

_____

Things that didn't get done today:

_____

_____

_____

_____

_____

_____

_____

_____

_____

_____

_____

_____

_____

DATE: _____ / _____ / _____

There's nothing like watching _____
(child's name)
make a new friend. The top places to meet
new pals are:

☐ Playground

☐ Music class

☐ Sandbox

☐ Other: _____

_____

_____

_____

_____

_____

_____

_____

_____

Here's when I'm happiest:

☐ Saturday lunch at a cute café. Cocoa for the
   kid(s). Coffee for me. We relax.

☐ Movie Mondays with snacks and juice boxes

☐ Hugs and snuggles just 'cause

☐ The table gets cleared, the beds get made—
   without me having to ask

☐ Other:_____

Notes:_____

_____

_____

_____

_____

_____

_____

_____

DATE: _____ / _____ / _____

Here's when I'm crankiest:

☐ When I've been woken up at 4 AM

☐ When I've spent the week with the stomach flu
   (mine or theirs)

☐ When they talk back

☐ When they lie

☐ Other: _____

Notes: _____

_____

_____

_____

_____

_____

_____

_____

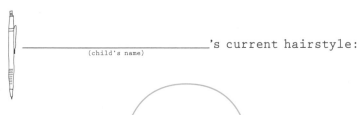

_____'s current hairstyle:
(child's name)

I like it:

☐ a little

☐ a lot

☐ very, very much

How many months since my kid's last

haircut:_____

My current hairstyle:

I like it:

☐ a little

☐ a lot

☐ very, very much

How many months since my last haircut:

_____ ; color: _____

I would like to take my significant other's Blackberry/iPhone and:

- [ ] Borrow it
- [ ] Read old e-mails
- [ ] Check the weather
- [ ] Throw it out the window
- [ ] Other: _____

Notes: _____

_____

_____

_____

_____

_____

_____

_____

DATE: _____/_____/_____

If I only had more time to capture every moment as a mom! Rank the following (with 1 being the activity I like least and 5 being the activity I like most):

_____ Scrapbooking

Why: _____

_____ Videotaping

Why: _____

_____ Blogging

Why: _____

_____ Organizing our digital pictures

Why: _____

_____ Updating the baby book

Why: _____

I am singularly happy when my
significant other:

☐ Plays jubilantly with our kids

☐ Laughs at my jokes

☐ Holds my hand during a scary scene
at the movies

☐ Plans a date night

☐ Other: _____

_____

_____

_____

_____

_____

_____

_____

DATE: _____ / _____ / _____

I am singularly unhappy when my
significant other:

☐ Feels upset about work

☐ Scolds the kids for something silly

☐ Tires of hearing me nag about stuff like
  fixing the toilet

☐ Farts loudly

☐ Other: _____

_____

_____

_____

_____

_____

_____

_____

_____

I'd describe my day today as:

- [ ] *Gone with the Wind*
- [ ] *War and Peace*
- [ ] *Crime and Punishment*
- [ ] *Pride and Prejudice*
- [ ] *The Beautiful and the Damned*
- [ ] *Brave New World*
- [ ] *Breakfast of Champions*
- [ ] *Dr. Jekyll and Mr. Hyde*
- [ ] Other:_____

_____

_____

_____

_____

_____

DATE: /   /

My biggest career/work goal is:

_____

_____

My biggest career/work concern is:

_____

_____

My signigicant other's biggest career/work
goal is:

_____

_____

My signigicant other's biggest career/work
concern is:

_____

_____

What I think of when I hear:

Dinner:_____

Holiday:_____

Fear:_____

Hope:_____

Good luck:_____

Guilty pleasure:_____

The future:_____

Notes:_____

_____

_____

_____

_____

_____

_____

DATE: _____ / _____ / _____

What _____ thinks of when
          (child's name)
I say:

Dinner:_____

Holiday:_____

Fear:_____

Hope:_____

Good luck:_____

Guilty pleasure:_____

The future:_____

Notes:_____

_____

_____

_____

_____

_____

Food = love? Maybe.
My "lovers"? I'll take:

☐ Chips and salsa

☐ Croissants

☐ Burgers and fries

☐ Ice cream (flavor:_____)

☐ Candy (favorite kind:_____)

☐ Other:_____

Notes:_____

_____

_____

_____

_____

_____

_____

Food = love? Maybe.
My kid(s) love:

☐ Mac-n-cheese

☐ Chicken fingers

☐ Hot dogs

☐ Burgers and fries

☐ Pasta with butter and cheese

☐ Other: _____

Notes: _____

_____

_____

_____

_____

_____

_____

Three things I wish for my kid(s):

1. _____

_____

2. _____

_____

3. _____

_____

Three things I wish for myself:

1. _____

_____

2. _____

_____

3. _____

_____

DATE: ___/___/___

The following tasks in our household are
generally taken care of by:

Takes out the trash:_____

Makes dinner:_____

Cleans the bathroom:_____

Mows the lawn:_____

Sweeps/vacuums:_____

Dusts:_____

Does the dishes:_____

Makes brunch on the weekends: _____

Grocery shops:_____

Other: _____

_____

_____

_____

_____

The last time I XXX texted my significant
other was:

☐ Yesterday

☐ This morning

☐ Never

☐ What's XXX?

☐ Other: _____

Notes: _____

_____

_____

_____

_____

_____

_____

I love lipstick! This is my signature shade:

(Place a kiss mark on this page or gently mark
in a sample of your lipstick shade. If you don't
wear lipstick, include a few sprays of your
trademark perfume or paint your favorite nail
polish color here. Don't forget to write down
the name.)

Today my kid(s) gave me:

- [ ] Kisses
- [ ] Attitude
- [ ] A story
- [ ] A hard time
- [ ] A cold
- [ ] A hug
- [ ] Other: _____

Notes: _____

_____

_____

_____

_____

_____

DATE: _____ / _____ / _____

Today I gave my kid(s):

☐ A hug

☐ Compliments

☐ A lecture

☐ A time-out

☐ A good dinner

☐ A piece of my mind

☐ Other: _____

Notes: _____

_____

_____

_____

_____

_____

_____

The biggest lesson my _____-year marriage has taught me:

_____

_____

_____

_____

_____

_____

Three things I've yet to learn:

1. _____

2. _____

3. _____

Notes: _____

_____

_____

The biggest lesson I've learned from my_____
years as a mom:

_____

_____

_____

_____

_____

_____

Three things I've yet to learn:

1. _____

2. _____

3. _____

Notes: _____

_____

_____

If someone wrote a song about me, it would be:

☐ *She's Got a Way* by Billy Joel

☐ *You're So Vain* by Carly Simon

☐ *Something in the Way She Moves* by James Taylor

☐ *Not Ready to Make Nice* by the Dixie Chicks

☐ All of the above

☐ Other: _____

Notes: _____

_____

_____

_____

_____

_____

_____

_____

DATE: _____ / _____ / _____

My significant other has still got it.

Smells like _____

Makes treats like _____

_____

Would be best person to be with on a desert island

because _____

_____

Laughs like _____

Other: _____

Notes: _____

_____

_____

_____

_____

_____

I've loved this phase that_____
(child's name)
is in. I call it_____.

Describe it: _____

_____

_____

_____

_____

_____

_____

_____

_____

_____

_____

_____

If I could have a uniform (no mom jeans for me), here's what I'd wear every day because I know it looks nice on me:

(Feel free to sketch your outfit here or paste in a magazine clipping or photograph.)

The three things that make me feel the most grounded:

1. _____

_____

2. _____

_____

3. _____

_____

The three things that (I think) make my kid(s) feel the most grounded:

1. _____

_____

2. _____

_____

3. _____

_____

DATE: _____ / _____ / _____

It takes a village to raise kids. Right now,
the people in my posse are:

- [ ] Mom/MIL
- [ ] Mom bloggers
- [ ] Friends in the neighborhood
- [ ] Moms from school
- [ ] Facebook group
- [ ] Knitting club
- [ ] Babysitter
- [ ] Village? What village?
- [ ] Other:_____

Notes: _____

_____

_____

_____

When I splurge, I go crazy buying...

Stuff for my kid(s) such as:

_____

_____

_____

_____

_____

_____

Stuff for my significant other such as:

_____

_____

_____

_____

_____

DATE: ___ / ___ / ___

I should splurge more on stuff for me such as:

_____

_____

_____

_____

_____

_____

_____

_____

_____

_____

_____

_____

_____

_____

I give myself an A+ as a wife when it comes to:

_____

_____

_____

I give myself an F as a wife when it comes to:

_____

_____

_____

Here's how I compensate for the F (sometimes):

_____

_____

_____

These days, the only times my significant other and I are alone is:

☐ When our kids are napping

☐ When our kids are at school

☐ At 3 AM

☐ Never

☐ Other:_____

The most recent place we kissed was in:

☐ The attic

☐ The car

☐ Bed

☐ An elevator

☐ The yard

☐ Other:_____

I'm going to do something charitable this month. This is the cause I care the most about:

_____

Why:_____

_____

What I'm going to do *now* to help: _____

_____

Notes:_____

_____

_____

_____

_____

_____

DATE: _____ / _____ / _____

I'm never too old to learn. I want to take
the following class this year:

☐ Beading

☐ Dance class

☐ Cooking

☐ Yoga/Pilates

☐ Art

☐ Career development

☐ Knitting

☐ A how-to-blog seminar

☐ Other:_____

Notes:_____

_____

_____

_____

My kid's favorite color is_____.
You'll find it cropping up in his/her:

☐ Clothes

☐ Artwork

☐ Accessories

☐ PJs

☐ Shoes

☐ Backpack

☐ Stuffed animals

☐ Foods

☐ Other:_____

Notes:_____

_____

_____

_____

DATE: _____ / _____ / _____

My favorite color is _____.

I love it so much because _____
_____.

This color is reflected in my:

☐ Clothes

☐ Interior décor

☐ Towels

☐ Accessories

☐ Shoes

☐ PJs

☐ Coffee mugs

☐ Artwork around the house

☐ Other: _____

Notes: _____

_____

Right now, _____'s nightly
(child's name)
rush-hour routine consists of:

6:00 PM: _____

_____

6:30 PM: _____

_____

7:00 PM: _____

_____

7:30 PM: _____

_____

8:00 PM: _____

_____

8:30 PM*: _____

_____

_____

*Is it bedtime for me yet? _____

DATE: _____ / _____ / _____

My AM routine never goes without a hitch.
Visualize me at:

6:00 AM: _____

_____

6:30 AM: _____

_____

7:00 AM: _____

_____

7:30 AM: _____

_____

8:00 AM: _____

_____

8:30 AM: _____

_____

9:00 AM: Day begins! _____

_____

The smell of _____ reminds me
most of my childhood.
When I hear this pop-culture reference

_____ ,

I feel like a teenager.
Ask me about college and the word that comes
to mind is_____ .
Favorite childhood game:_____
Favorite band from my teenage years:

_____

Favorite food I can remember growing up:

_____

Other:_____

_____

_____

DATE: ____/____/_____

The most adorable thing about _____
(child's name)

is _____.

The most aggravating thing about _____
(child's name)

is _____.

The most surprising thing about _____
(child's name)

is _____.

The most silly thing about _____
(child's name)

is _____.

The most wonderful thing about _____
(child's name)

is _____

_____

_____

_____

_____

When I wake up and think about work, the first thing that comes to mind is:

☐ I'm excited—I'm doing what I always dreamed of

☐ I'm bored to tears—this isn't for me

☐ I want to go back to sleep

☐ I know it could be worse

☐ I need a career counselor

☐ Other: _____

Notes: _____

_____

_____

_____

_____

_____

_____

DATE: _____ / _____ / _____

If my significant other and I had more time
to talk, this is what I'd say about how
I'm feeling right now—about our life, our
marriage, our kids:

_____

_____

_____

_____

_____

_____

_____

_____

_____

_____

_____

_____

_____

Three ways I'm mothering the way my mom did:

1. _____

_____

2. _____

_____

3. _____

_____

And three ways I'm taking a completely
different path from my mom:

1. _____

_____

2. _____

_____

3. _____

_____

DATE: _____ / _____ / _____

Since I've become a mom, the part of my body
I'm happiest with is _____
_____.

My _____could use
a little work.

Notes: _____
_____
_____
_____
_____
_____
_____
_____
_____
_____

_____'s thumbprint art!
(child's name)

(Put your child's thumbprint on this page and make
an illustration out of it.)

My thumbprint art!

(Put your thumbprint on this page and make an illustration out of it.)

I wish I could do the following things as well as my significant other can:

☐ Caulk a bathtub

☐ Whistle a tune

☐ Ski

☐ Grill a steak

☐ Other: _____

Notes: _____

_____

_____

_____

_____

_____

_____

DATE: _____ / _____ / _____

Hands down, I know I'm better at the following
things than my significant other is:

☐ Baking cookies

☐ Comforting the kids when they get hurt

☐ Giving back rubs

☐ Talking about "issues"

☐ Other: _____

Notes: _____

_____

_____

_____

_____

_____

_____

_____

I know I should be grateful that I don't have
to pound my clothing on a rock to clean it,
but laundry stresses me out.

I would like to invent _____
to make this task easier.

And, speaking of easier, I wouldn't mind
having a contraption around the house to do
the following things:

1. _____

2. _____

3. _____

4. _____

5. _____

Notes: _____

_____

_____

When it comes to being a mom, I've found my gut instinct is usually right. For example:

_____

_____

_____

_____

_____

_____

_____

_____

_____

_____

_____

_____

The letters PTA make me think of:

☐ Petulant Tyrannical Adults

☐ *Knots Landing*

☐ *Election*

☐ Lots of angry women in one room

☐ Powerful women making positive things happen
at my child's school

☐ Other: _____

Notes: _____

_____

_____

_____

_____

_____

_____

DATE: _____ / _____ / _____

This was a surprisingly good day because:

_____

_____

_____

_____

_____

_____

_____

_____

_____

_____

_____

_____

_____

_____

_____

_____

_____

How I would describe myself in one adjective:

_____

How I would describe myself in one verb:

_____

How I would describe myself in one superlative:

_____

OK, here's more on how I would describe my

whole self:_____

_____

_____

_____

_____

_____

_____

_____

DATE: _____ / _____ / _____

How I would describe _____
                                    (child's name)

in one adjective: _____

How I would describe _____
                                    (child's name)

in one verb: _____

How I would describe _____
                                    (child's name)

in one superlative: _____

A bit more bragging about my child:

_____

_____

_____

_____

_____

_____

_____

_____

Rate the following from 1 (least annoying) to 5 (most annoying). It irritates me when a mom I once liked morphs into a frenemom by:

_____Disciplining my child

_____Making playdates and then canceling them last minute

_____Complaining about her busy schedule

_____Fawning about her child's latest accomplishments ad nauseum

_____Other:_____

Vent here:
_____
_____
_____
_____
_____
_____
_____

DATE: ___ / ___ / ___

The following five things went well today:

1. _____

2. _____

3. _____

4. _____

5. _____

Notes: _____

_____

_____

_____

_____

_____

_____

_____

_____